Manifestes
1

Javier Fernández Contreras
Manifesto of Interiors: Thinking in the Expanded Media

MANIFESTO OF INTERIORS	7
LABORATORIES OF MODERNITY	21
THINKING IN THE EXPANDED MEDIA	53

1

MANIFESTO OF INTERIORS

'Between words and objects one can create new relations...'[1]

René Magritte

---

[1] 'Between words and objects one can create new relations and specify characteristics of language and objects generally ignored in everyday life.' René Magritte quoted in Foucault, 1983, p.38

When in 1929 René Magritte presented the work *Ceci n'est pas une pipe*, he essentially revealed, apart from a fascination with the seduction of images, the role of art as an intermediary between the world and the observer. Aware that interferences may arise in the representation of things, he articulated a manifesto as evident as it was provocative: images of things are not things themselves, but rather representations, and as such they do not need to respect the same rules.

The reference to Magritte's painting is revealing in the contemporary world, in which contact with architecture is no longer fully the result of direct experience, having been gradually replaced by a 'mediated experience'. The first question that should therefore be asked when speaking of interior design nowadays is: which media construct the relationship between interior spaces and their perception, between physical reality and how it is thought about?

This question addresses, as in the case of Magritte's painting, the format of representation itself. Ultimately, what is the medium (or media) of interior architecture today? The issue is epistemological and affects how the discipline is envisioned.

This diagram means essentially three things:
1) The direct experience of space is a fragment of a larger, complex whole.
2) The articulation between physical and mediated spaces defines contemporary interiors.
3) The internet and online platforms amplify the complexity of this diagram n-fold.

INTERIOR SPACE

Perspective drawing	Painting	Theatre	Conversation	Exhibition
Orthographic drawing	Photography	Cinema	Radio	Installation
Diagram	Illustration	TV	Music	Performance
Model/Mock-up	Collage	Cartoon	Literature	
Software 2/3D - BIM	Comic	Videogame	Magazine	
Digital Reality			Publicity	
		(n) Online		Direct Experience
		...		

PERCEPTION – THINKING

Medium has two plurals, *media* and *mediums*. While there is some liminal area between them, media is mainly used in reference to communications—publishing, advertising, broadcasting, streaming—whereas *medium/s* traditionally refers to the materials, techniques, and technologies associated with particular representations of information and knowledge.

The entanglements of these definitions constitute an epistemological debate in itself, from the prosthetic thinking of Marshall McLuhan in the 1960s, envisioning media as 'extensions of men',[2] to contemporary visions of authors such as Lisa Gitelman, defining them as 'socially realised structures of communication',[3] to insist upon the relation between technology, cultural context, and popular ontology of representation. To a certain extent, media can be considered a relational term, whereas *medium/s* is structurally linear.

The thinking of interior architecture nowadays is produced through different media and systems of representation. Texts, drawings, photographs, films, and their endless crossovers on online platforms have replaced in many cases the physical experience of space. This matters because contemporary thinking is relational. When envisioning, talking, and reflecting upon space, society does not discriminate between different disciplines. Designers, artists, filmmakers, programmers, or publicists all inform the agency of

2   McLuhan, 1964
3   Gitelman, 2006, p.7

contemporary interiors through multiple formats, temporalities, and intersections.

The origins of this cross-fertilisation, by which different disciplines influence the agency of space design, can be traced back to the Renaissance. Whereas the beginning of modern philosophy is situated in the 17th century with René Descartes, it is clear that the image of the modern world emerges in the era of Italian humanism and the Renaissance. This is relevant because the reasoning that informed this 'modern image' was produced through a new apparatus of systems of spatial representation that were both shaped and developed through multiple transversal associations that blurred their disciplinary borders.

Spanning a timeframe between 1420 and 1590, the Renaissance witnessed the successive discovery of linear perspective in architecture and painting, the institutionalisation of the use of orthographic projections in architectural drawing, the development of models and set designs for theatre, and the transition from inaccurate to 'photographic' painting, i.e., the capacity to capture precisely three-dimensional reality on a flat, two-dimensional surface. The history of each system of representation can be traced back independently, but it is their cross-fertilisation that anticipates—or informs—modern thinking.

Linear perspective was devised by Filippo Brunelleschi between 1415 and 1420 through a series of graphic experiments conducted in Florence,

[Fig. 1] **Villa Almerico (Villa Rotunda)** from: Andrea Palladio. *I quattro libri dell'architettura* (Book 2, 19), 1570

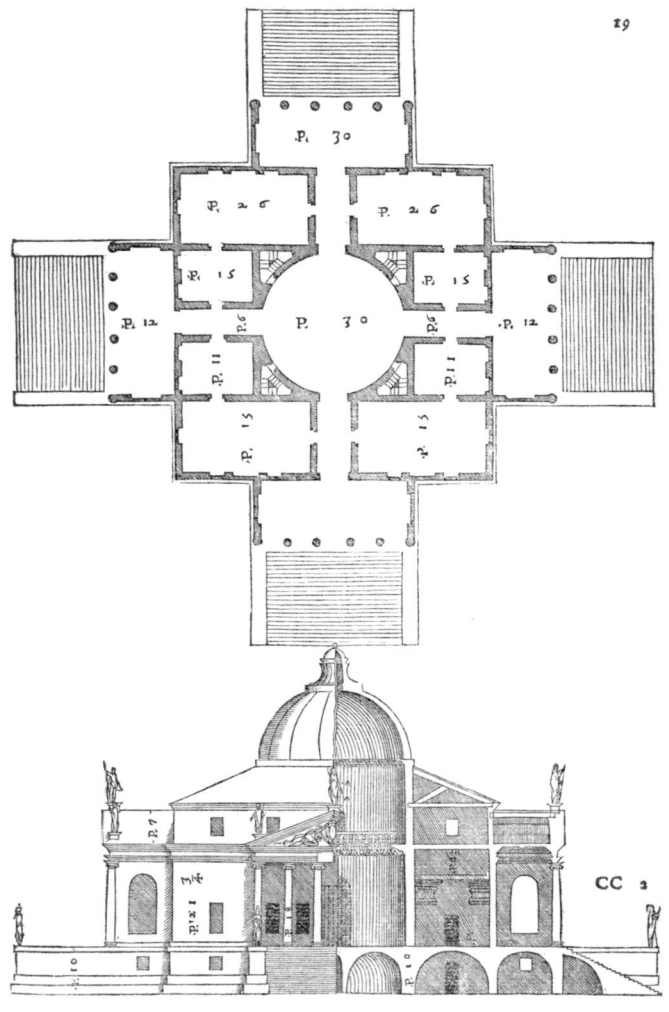

which culminated in a famed public demonstration in front of the Baptistery comparing the reflection of his one-point perspective drawing on a mirror with the actual building. The full system was later documented by Leon Battista Alberti in his 1435 treatise *Della Pittura*, which prompted nearly every artist in Florence and in Italy to use geometrical perspective in their paintings thereafter, in what is considered one of the major points of inflexion in the history of Western art and spatial thinking.

Orthographic projections—plan, section, elevation—had been used independently for centuries, but their combined use as a standard for architectural representation was progressively institutionalised in the 15th and 16th centuries with the drawings of Leon Battista Alberti and Andrea Palladio, becoming a graphic canon that has dominated architectural conventions for centuries. The radical consequences of this shift for architectural thinking have been discussed by Robin Evans in his seminal book *The Projective Cast: Architecture and its Three Geometries*, published in 1995. Evans argues that, despite its rejection of tradition and classicism, architecture was the sole discipline that did not question its representation codes in the early 20th century avant-garde, which means spatial representation mechanisms can be read seamlessly from the Renaissance into Modernism: 'The triumvirate of plan, elevation, and section were not identified as part of the problem and so continued as

working desiderata of the profession. [...] Modern painters attacked perspective vociferously, dubbed it a mere convention, removed evidence of it from their work, and claimed that vision itself was not perspectival. For them the dominant means of representation was an issue, for modern architects apparently not.'[4]

The same can be argued for models, whose regular use in various scales came to prominence in the same historic context of 15th-century Italy and reaches into the present, having gained progressive objecthood and disciplinary autonomy in recent decades. As Thea Brejzek and Lawrence Wallen propose in the 2018 book *The Model as Performance*, the Italian Renaissance saw the simultaneous development of the use of models in architecture and theatre, arguing that their articulation was critical in the development of new spatial practices.[5] These experiments broached issues such as the relationship between the objecthood and representational condition of models, their epistemic autonomy and independence from full-size architecture, and their association with the human body and sense of visual inhabitation, exploring the agency of scale in the construction of space.

Projects such as Andrea Palladio's Teatro Olimpico (1580-85) and Vincenzo Scamozzi's Teatro all'Antica (1588-90)

[Fig. 2] **Vincenzo Scamozzi. Teatro all'Antica, 1588-1590. Modern reconstruction of Scamozzi's original work**

4   Evans, 1995, p.119
5   Brejzek and Wallen, 2018

Manifesto of Interiors   15

[Fig. 3] **Dieric Bouts.** *The Last Supper.* 1464-1468

created immersive 1:1 models with their set designs. The stage scenography of both schemes is simultaneously representational (directly alluding to urban scenarios), manipulative (deforming them both visually and spatially), and autonomous (becoming both the content and the objective of their own representation). Moreover, both could only be designed combining the mechanisms of orthographic projections with linear perspective and model making, blurring representational and, more importantly, disciplinary boundaries between architectural and scenic design. As Scamozzi's drawings for the Teatro all'Antica show, the set was drawn not as a separate element or addition but as part of the original architectural plan-section-elevation, attesting to their conceptual unity and creating new practices of space design that had to be, literally, performed.[6] The Renaissance therefore marks a critical moment in the history of spatial design, when different systems of representation begin to influence each other, and in that it heralds, albeit with fewer means, the contemporary era.

The scope of this epistemological shift goes beyond architecture and can easily be recognised in other coetaneous revolutions affecting other disciplines. As explained by David Hockney in his seminal work *Secret Knowledge: Rediscovering the Lost Techniques of the Old Masters*, first published in 2001, a similar relational way of thinking can be recognised in painting. According to the au-

6 *Ibid.*

thor, the incorporation of linear perspective into Western painting cannot be separated from the use of optical instruments (curved mirrors, *camera obscura*) to fix the image of things on the flat surface of the canvas.[7] Aside from the technical achievements this implied, it meant a radical shift in spatial thinking, allowing for the combination of different diachronic elements and spaces on the synchronic surface of the canvas. As Hockney explains in relation to Dieric Bouts' painting *The Last Supper*, the characters and objects assembled in the painting were collaged through separate mirror-lens views.[8] The capacity to see things and objects projected and decontextualised on a flat surface is, in Hockney's words, 'photographic', or when things move, as in his recreation of Sánchez Cotán's *Quince, Cabbage, Melon and Cucumber*, a 'television picture.'[9]

The Renaissance thus represents the first historic period when the quantity and relational use of different systems of representation increase significantly. Space-model, space-theatre, space-painting, the set designs by Palladio and Scamozzi, and the paintings analysed by Hockney share a capacity to produce spaces that are both representational and performative, physical and mediated. They all imply an understanding of space as physically ephemeral and representa-

---

7 Hockney, 2006
8 *Ibid.*, p.86-89
9 *David Hockney: Secret Knowledge*, directed by Randall Wright (BBC Production, 2001), 30'35"

tionally durable. In that sense, they anticipate the modern understanding of interiors as media and fundamentally multiply the directions in which representation, as tool and practice, operates.

2

LABORATORIES OF MODERNITY

'There are liquids which, cubic inch for cubic inch, are heavier than many solids, but we are inclined nonetheless to visualize them all as lighter, less "weighty" than everything solid. We associate "lightness" or "weightlessness" with mobility and inconstancy: we know from practice that the lighter we travel the easier and faster we move.
These are reasons to consider "fluidity" or "liquidity" as fitting metaphors when we wish to grasp the nature of the present, in many ways *novel,* phase in the history of modernity.'[10]

Zygmunt Bauman

---

10   Bauman, 2000, p.2

Interior spaces are nowadays laboratories of modernity. Whether through renovation projects, temporary scenography, or emergency setups, interiors have become an endless arena for the exploration of social, environmental, and political agendas that transform the contemporary condition from within.

In the book *Liquid Modernity*, first published in 2000, philosopher Zygmunt Bauman defends the contemporary era as a continuation or late development of early modernity. As opposed to 'postmodern', he suggests the notion of 'liquid' to better epitomise the condition of constant change and displacement within contemporary societies. According to Bauman, modernity has always been dichotomous. On the one hand, it is characterised by an idea and ideal of perfection and order—the image of an improved world as an objective: rational, civilised, and stable in its social, political, and economic organisation. On the other, it is defined by an agenda of radical change to achieve this improved state by melting and destroying old concepts and traditions. The main difference between the first 'solid' phase and the contemporary 'liquid' phase of modernity is in the nature of change itself. Early modernity is predicated on the idea of a final destination, 'solidity which one could trust and rely upon and which would make the world predictable and therefore manageable',[11] whereas liquid modernity makes of change and transiency its perpetual state. Later in his career he paralleled this liquid state with what he called *the tourist syndrome* to refer to 'the looseness of ties with a place—physical, geographical, social.'[12]

This dichotomous nature is directly related to the evolution of architecture in the last century. In the early 20th century, architectural modernity was significantly associated with the systematisation of order, urban planning, and the territorial expansion of cities, a process that has left its mark on contemporary cities and societies. Parallel to the institutionalisation of modern interiors by means of international exhibitions, new department stores, and mass media, it was urban planning, associated with ideas of order and functionalism, that dominated the agenda of architectural discourse. Today, especially in the West, most buildings and urban environments have already been developed and often have a heritage listing. Hence, the laboratory for architectural experimentation has shifted towards the transformation of interior spaces, both permanent and ephemeral. Whether it is in the exploration of new domesticities, creative industries, or cultural premises, all transformations in contemporary societies are linked to constantly changing interior spaces, while the façades of the buildings remain the same.

In recent decades, the increase in mobility, displacement, and physical instability has coexisted with the rise in heritage preservation, which

11   *Ibid.* p.3
12   Franklin, 2003, p.207

has significantly affected architectural tectonics, mainly load-bearing structures and façades, a process which has turned the interior into a domain of freedom and experimentation for new architectural agendas. Contemporary interiors are flexible, ephemeral, transient, and easily updated, or 'liquid' to use Bauman's term, whereas exteriors/façades are increasingly regulated, protected, 'solid'.

This has produced a schism that is articulating, for the first time in the history of the discipline, first the emancipation and subsequently the autonomy of the realm of interior architecture. The schism between inside and outside has established interiors as flexible and deregulated domains, changing much more rapidly according to mutations in contemporary societies. Transformations are associated with constantly changing interiors, such as transient domestic spaces, public spaces in derelict buildings, non-places in transport or commercial facilities, and experimental programs in existing structures. Today, interior architecture is, by definition, a laboratory of late modernity; it is the real place of production of contemporaneity. In these territories, interior architects build contemporary societies through interior spaces: the articulation of scenarios of equality, the reduction of energy consumption, the integration of social minorities, or the respect for sexual, political, and religious diversity are social constructs linked

[Fig. 4] Attributed to Bramante (1444-1514), drawing of ancient ruins

to the techniques, materials, and iconographies of contemporary interiors.

This schism is also mediated. In 'The Archaeology of Section',[13] Jacques Guillerme and Hélène Vérin trace the origins of the architectural section back to the observation and drawing of ruins in the 16th century, particularly of Roman ruins. As the illustrations of Bramante or Sangallo show, the ruin is the sole architectural type before modernism that allows a simultaneous view of section profile and inside elevation. The capacity to visualise interiors with a certain degree of graphic autonomy might have produced an operative independence in the relationship to their exterior counterparts. No wonder that *façadism*, a practice by which architectural elevations are detached from their corresponding interiors, flourished in the same period, as exemplified by the Palazzo della Ragione in Vicenza, which in 1549 was refronted by Andrea Palladio, who erected a classical façade in front of an earlier medieval market hall.[14]

The practice was common across different historical periods and locations, as illustrated by examples as diverse as the Santiago de Compostela Cathedral (a temple with a baroque façade superimposed on a Romanic portico) or the Town Hall of Utrecht (an ensemble of medieval constructions whose façades evolved autonomously from the Renaissance to the 20th century). By the 18th century the autonomy of the façade was commonplace in major urban operations in Europe. This was clear for architect John Wood the Younger, who designed the Royal Crescent in Bath between 1767 and 1775 as a 150-metre-long façade with free interiors. The façade was built as a self-standing masonry wall whose interiors were subsequently customised by users and inhabitants. Here the elevation was the infrastructure to which autonomous spaces could be attached, an intellectual operation that precedes 20th-century architectural utopias such as Megastructures, Japanese Metabolism, and the urban postulates of postwar Europe.[15]

It is interesting to note that John Wood belonged to a time whose architectural ethos was largely shaped by the Grand Tour, originally a trip undertaken by upper-class Englishmen across Central Europe and Italy whose record was shaped through drawing and sketching. The 'image' of architecture at that time was therefore shaped by classic treatises and published accounts of travellers' visits to classical monuments and ruins, along with individual sketches and notebooks that could circulate informally. Treatises were formal, consistent, and canonical, whereas private drawings were fragmentary and dispersed. And yet they institutionalised the schism of their time, in which each generation of travelers observed the same ruins but produced different drawings.

---

13 Guillerme and Vérin, 1989
14 Richards, 1994, p.24
15 Sánchez García, 2016, p.197-212

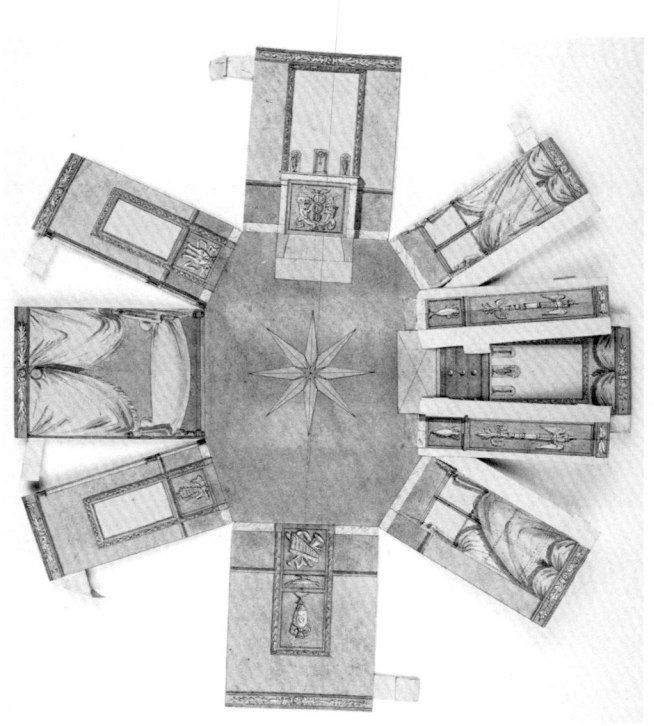

How then did interiors become autonomous or 'liquid' to use Bauman's term? This might arguably be related to drawing. In 'The Developed Surface', Robin Evans analyses the graphic method of representing rooms with the walls folded out as adjacent surfaces in mid-18th-century Britain. Favored by Robert Adam—a Grand Tour traveller—in his commissions, the technique 'became a way of turning architecture inside-out, so that internal rather than external elevations were shown.'[16] The practice became popular in other countries and some architects even used the drawing as an intermediate model, such as Pierre-François-Léonard Fontaine, who added tabs to fasten the paper pieces and form up dollhouse-like objects.[17]

Panelling, carpets, drapes, built-in furniture, mobile furniture—these drawings and models produced a total disengagement of domestic interiors from architectural tectonics, namely the load-bearing structures, and masonry walls. No wonder that, in their very autonomy, interiors became decontextualised and mobile. The 19th century saw the simultaneous development of a market for salvaged domestic interiors and the emergence of Period Rooms,[18] a form of museum display in which works of art of various

[Fig. 5] Pierre-François-Léonard Fontaine. Drawing model (possibly for Empress Josephine's bedroom at Fontainebleau). 1804

16   Evans, 1997, p.203
17   Moon, 2019
18   For a critical inquiry into the relationship between Period Rooms and the market for salvaged architecture interiors in 19th century Britain and America, see: Harris, 2007.

Laboratories of Modernity

genres, handicrafts, and furniture were exhibited in domestic-like rooms appointed with original finishings, showing an ideal overall picture of an era. The museography of the room, different to the room per se, became a medium in itself.

The more interiors were decontextualised, documented, and preserved in museums, the more foreign they became to their original domain, i.e., architecture. And again, a major medium disruption became critical to the further institutionalisation of this process. The centrality of photography, a 19th-century invention, in the preservation of façades and the schism between inside and outside remains a critical endeavour in architectural theory. Façades were exterior, public, and photographed, whereas private interiors remained for decades—before the internet—uncirculated, unregistered, and *unimaged*. The potential of this tension between private spaces and visualised interiors was explored by avant-garde artists and designers long before the digital era.

In 1913 Pablo Picasso sequentially photographed the work *Construction with Guitar Player* in his Paris studio in an active process mixing painting, collage, spatial composition, and photography in different iterations. In the first image, a partially painted canvas is combined with a real guitar in a visual composition that includes the space of the room, indicating that painting and collage have been assembled in a larger photographic representation. In the second and third images, Picasso cuts the photograph and pastes it

[Fig. 6] **Pablo Picasso.** *Composition with 'Construction with Guitar Player'.* 1913

[Fig. 7] **Pablo Picasso.** *Photographic Composition with 'Construction with Guitar Player'.* 1913

onto a white canvas. The profiles of the cropped fragments produce their own autonomous figure, which integrates the pictorial (canvas), the photographic (table and bottle), the collage (guitar), and finally the space of the room in the same cut to form a new composition.[19]

The sequence of images favours an oscillation of perception between the real space of the room and the virtual domain of the pictorial. Picasso was one of the first artists to envision artistic practice as the intersection of a number of systems of representation such as painting, collage, photography, and spatial design in successive iterations and manipulations. He not only reshaped traditional formats (painting), embraced contemporary ones (photography), and created new ones (collage), but more importantly articulated them in a relational way that anticipated contemporaneity.

In that sense, Le Corbusier can arguably be considered the architectural counterpart of Picasso, as the first modern architect to clearly understand that architecture had shifted from being just a physical construct to becoming inseparable from its construction as media, as explained by Beatriz Colomina in *Privacy and Publicity*, one of the most influential books on architectural theory since its publication in 1994. Through the constant editing of photography (elimination of context, emphasis on architecture as autonomous object), the inclusion of publicity mechanisms in

19 Rojo, 2015, p.278-370

architectural theory (slogans, visual reading of juxtaposed images), and a cinematographic sense of space (ramps and promenades that articulate 'montaged' spaces), Le Corbusier used media not to neutrally represent reality, but to fabricate new forms—and formats—of architectural reality. As Colomina argues, 'In Paris, more precisely with the experience of *L'Esprit nouveau*, he came to understand the press, the printed media, not only as a medium for the cultural diffusion of something previously existing but also as a context of production with its own autonomy.'[20]

This is a radical shift from the pre-modernist format of architectural theory and practice. From Vitruvius in classical antiquity to J.-N.-L. Durand in Neoclassicism, one could argue that architectural theory had focused for centuries on the production—as idea and project—of physical spaces. Not for Le Corbusier. Despite his considerable built oeuvre, he was an architect of images as much as tectonics; probably the first who succeeded in uniting these two categories, using reality to produce images and vice versa. He belonged to a time and ethos where technical innovations were as important as the fabrication of new realities that were performed in the space of representation. Architecture could not thereafter be understood merely as a collection of physical events, it was also to be recognised as a collection of mediated realities.

20 Colomina, 1994, p.104

[Fig. 8] *The Seven Year Itch.* Directed by Billy Wilder. 1955

Laboratories of Modernity   35

Since the beginning of the 20th century, the progressive institutionalisation of the modern interior was promoted through exhibitions, advertising, and other media, rarely existing in an absolute form. As Penny Sparke explains in the 2008 book, *The Modern Interior*, the transition from Victorian to Modern style led by Le Corbusier and similar protagonists of the Modern Movement (Adolf Loos, Frank Lloyd Wright, Charlotte Perriand, Josef Frank, Marcel Breuer, Lilly Reich, Mies van der Rohe, Charles and Ray Eames) was only made possible by the implementation of a whole apparatus of complementary means of production and mass media, able to construct an entirely new *lifestyle*, a word scarcely used in the 'official' history of modern architecture, yet critical to understanding it.[21] Not only were exhibitions, international trade fairs, and commercial catalogues incorporated into the conception of novel spaces, so was cinema. Hollywood films such as *The Kiss* (1929) and *Grand Hotel* (1932), both starring Greta Garbo, wooed mass audiences and designers through their use of stylish, streamlined modern interiors. As Sparke explains, 'Film interiors were hugely influential. A bedroom set in *The Kiss* reap-

[Fig. 9] Heinrich Himmler and Albert Speer (right) in front of a North-South Axis model, Berlin, 1941

21 'Model domestic interiors were presented as static images and spaces, complete with puffed-up cushions. Real lives, in that context, were replaced by the modern, mass media-dependent notion of "lifestyles", the idealised versions, that is, of the lives that people actually lead.' Sparke, 2008, p.57

Laboratories of Modernity

peared, for instance, in a bedroom design created by John Wellborn Root which was shown at the *Architect and the Industrial Arts* exhibition held in New York's Metropolitan Museum of Art in the same year the film was released.'[22]

Even though new aesthetics could easily be imagined in cinematography, both visual and non-visual aspects such as comfort, energy, and air conditioning were equally conveyed through film interiors. This affected not only the aesthetic construction of the modern interior but also its inhabitation and comfort through the space of the screen, in the creation of new lifestyles, as can be seen in Billy Wilder's *The Seven Year Itch* (1955), starring Marilyn Monroe as a single tenant who, in the torrid New York summer, strikes up a friendship with her downstairs neighbor through her interest in his air-conditioned apartment. Widely recognised as one of the most influential films of post-war sexual liberation, it was also one of the first to integrate air conditioning as an object of desire, both atmospheric and physical, always displayed at the centre of the living room. The film epitomises the paradigm shift regarding comfort in the metropolis, where the centrality of the fireplace in the domestic interior (winter paradigm: warm chimney, opaque back wall) is replaced with that of air conditioning (summer paradigm: cooling equipment, transparent window).

In the first half of the 20th century, cinema became the domain for the construction not only

[22] *Ibid.*, p.72

[Fig. 10] **Piet Mondrian.**
Compositie in kleur A. 1917

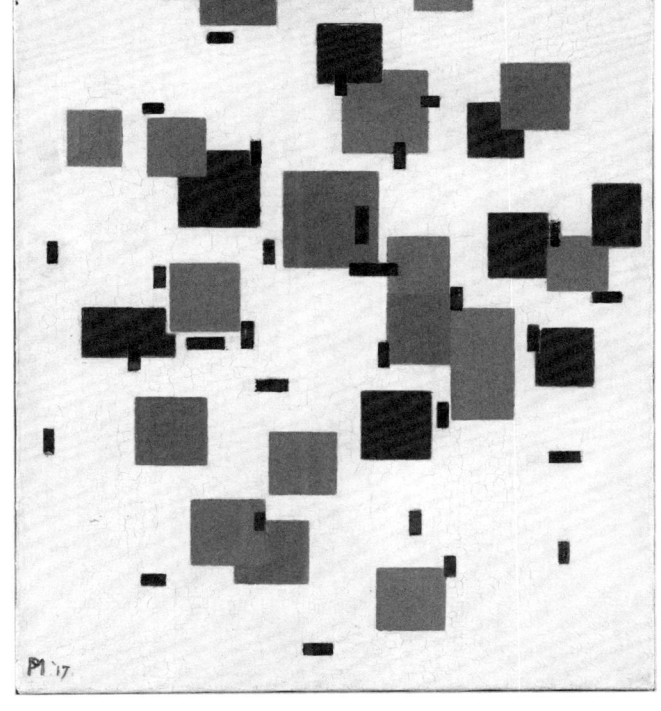

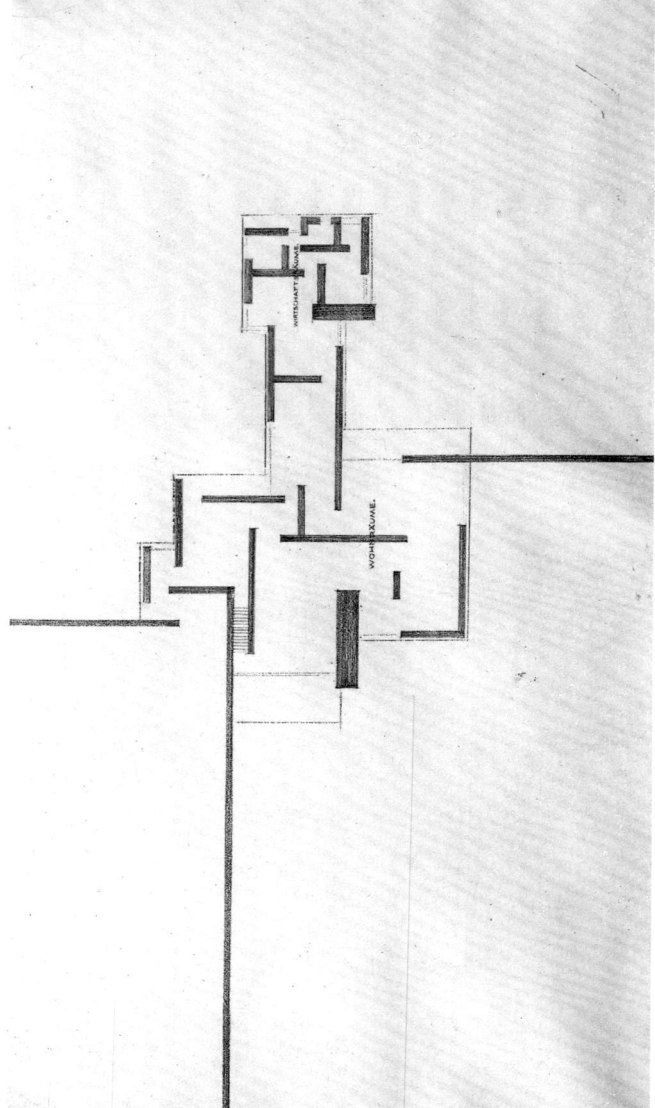

of new lifestyles but also of utopian and dystopian fictions of social realities through the audio-visual. The assembly of space, time, and representation was explored in manifold directions, from the early technical and montage experiments of the Russian pioneers (Dziga Vertov, Sergei Eisenstein) to the expressionist scenography of German films (Fritz Lang, Robert Wiene). Probably the most radical examples were those of political propaganda, where the boundaries between reality and fiction were challenged, using fiction to fabricate new realities. A case in point is Nazi Germany's use of detailed architectural scale models that were publicised not only via print media but also via film, blurring distinctions between built reality and dystopian future. Models were used notably in the 1939 Ufa newsreel *Das Wort aus Stein,* being inserted and montaged within real urban scenes in documentary style so that the spectator could not differentiate between the buildings' present and future state; between the reality of power and its representation through media.[23]

For interiors, these experiments implied three simultaneous revolutions:

1. The public/private dichotomy was replaced by that of mediated/non-mediated.
2. Spaces, in their idea, agency, and performance, gradually became hubs articulating physical and virtual domains.

[Fig. 11] Mies van der Rohe. Brick Country House. 1923

23 Brejzek and Wallen, *op. cit.*, p.113

3. Fiction, reality, and representation began to mutually inform one another, rendering their borders ambiguous.

The implications of this paradigm shift not only affected the aesthetics of interiors but addressed profound structural and topological transformations beyond the visual and iconographic convergence described by Colomina and Sparke. In this sense, the transfers between the art of the avant-garde and the structure of modern space, especially as codified in the plans of Le Corbusier and Mies van der Rohe, are remarkable.

The influence of the Dutch artistic avant-garde, namely *de Stijl*, in Mies' floor plans has been cited since the first monographic exhibition of his work at MoMA in 1947. Curated by Philip Johnson, who had previously introduced modern architecture to America through the 1932 exhibition *The International Style*, the catalogue discussed the cross-fertilisation between abstract pictorial surfaces and tectonic structures: 'Never in history had architecture been so influenced by painting. [...] Unlike Expressionism, which petered out in the 1920s, both *de Stijl* and Constructivism were to be assimilated by what has since become known as "modern architecture".'[24] For Mies, this was particularly recognisable in the period between 1919 and 1925, when he was involved in complementary activities such as architectural design, exhibition organisation, and the-

24 Johnson, 1947, p.21

[Fig. 12] **Enric Miralles, Eva Prats. 'How to Lay Out a Croissant. Horizontal Equilibrium'.** *El Croquis* N. 49/50, 1991, p.240-241

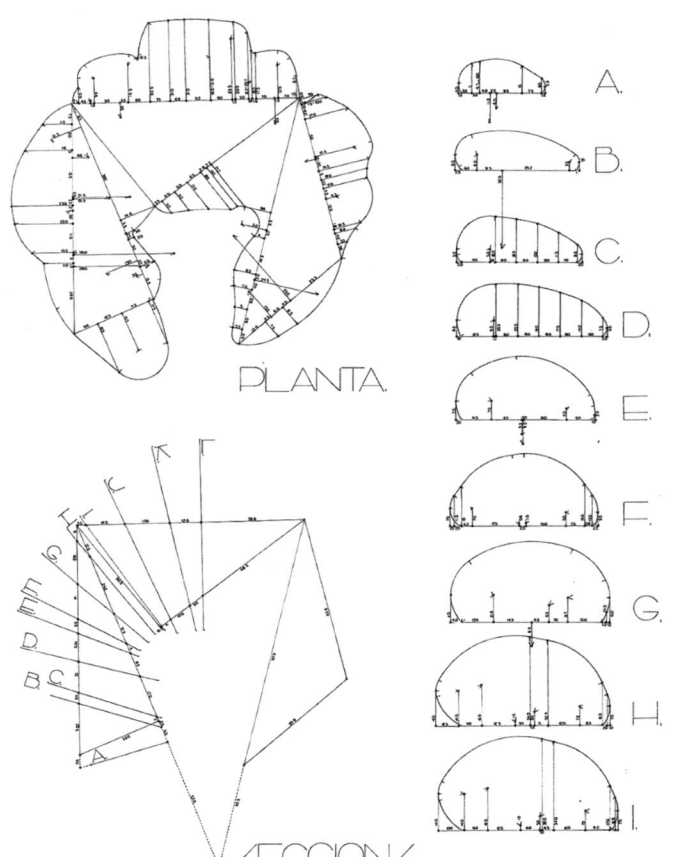

ory writing in the magazine *G*, which had a strong *de Stijl* influence. Those were experimental years for the architect, when he conceived the visionary schemes that would set the basis of his spatial grammar through projects such as the brick country house, whose built counterpart would be the Barcelona Pavilion, erected in 1929 for the World Expo. In both projects, the break-up of the architectural box and the centripetal distribution of separate walls alludes to the geometric influence of the work of Mondrian, Van Doesburg, and other *de Stijl* members, which permeates the architectural floor plan.

As for Le Corbusier, the structural revolutions introduced by his conceptualisation of the free plan, namely the dissociation of the load-bearing column grid from the plasticity of the partition walls, cannot be separated from his artistic practice, mainly purist painting. Purism was a form of art developed by the architect with artist Amédée Ozenfant in the 1920s, which advocated the use of recurrent voluptuously shaped *object types* (bottles, string instruments, plates), arranged in an orderly fashion in elementary compositions devoid of any detail within the rectangular frame of the canvas. Floating curve against rectangle, figure against background, the identification of these geometric objects with curvilinear room types, mainly to address toilets and ancillary spaces, indicates a direct transfer from painting to architecture,

[Fig. 13] Rem Koolhaas/OMA. Y2K House. 1998

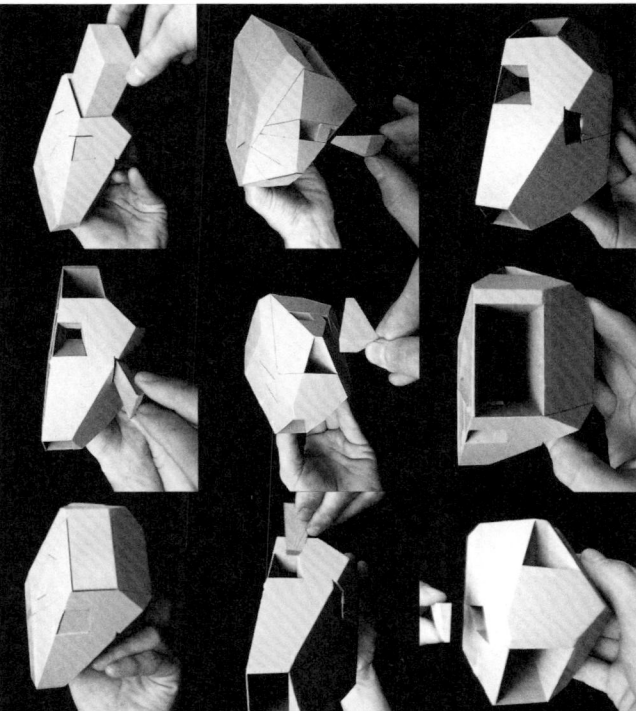

the evolution of which extends through the architect's career. When, after breaking from Ozenfant in 1925, Le Corbusier evolved away from Purism in favor of other topics such as the *mariage de contours* (in which a single line draws two profiles belonging to different figures that overlap and intersect), curves were progressively extended to structure the entire plan of projects such as the Ronchamp Chapel or the Carpenter Center.

The potential of incorporating pictorial patterns into architecture was therefore heavily explored in the early decades of the 20th century by modern architects, asserting that anything drawn with geometric precision could structure the plan and, consequently, space. In a more recent example, one can see the evolution of Enric Miralles' architecture through the same principles. In 1991, Miralles published with then-collaborator Eva Prats a seminal article, 'How to Lay out a Croissant', where they explained the mechanisms by which to draw with exactitude a croissant's irregular figure in what unexpectedly became a geometric manifesto.[25] Many projects designed by Miralles with partner Benedetta Tagliabue in the 1990s can be read as the incorporation of extrinsic geometries into the architectural plan, such as the Parc in Mollet del Vallès, where the geometry of gardens and pavements was literally imported from David Hockney paintings, or the Smart showroom project, in which the ultrasounds

25   Miralles and Prats, 1991

of Miralles/Tagliabue's first daughter were used to formalise the outline of the plan.[26]

A similar reading in volumetric terms can be recognised in Rem Koolhaas' project for the concert hall Casa da Musica in Porto, a literal blow-up of a smaller project by OMA that was never built, the Y2K house. In 1999, Koolhaas explained the project in a lecture explicitly called *Transformations*, referring to the cynicism but also efficiency of the transfer from one model to another in terms that, to a certain extent, epitomise the architecture of the end of the 1990s in its operative capacity to disengage form from function, geometry from volume, and scale from matter: 'The more we thought about it and the more we looked—because at this point the visual becomes the dominant force—the more appealing it became to simply shift scales and use all the earlier research as a form of immediacy.'[27]

This does not mean a reductionism of architectural elements, nor an inverted postmodernism of symbols applied to the floor plan or the volume, but rather a scalelessness and relational thinking in space design that defines contemporaneity. Similar displacements can be seen historically in the Greek temple—whose typological origin is a literal scale-up of small timber-frame structures to monumentalised stone construction—or in the inhabited ruin, i.e., the Diocletian Palace, one of the most significant historic examples of how in-

26 Contreras, 2020, p.60-69
27 Koolhaas, 2000, p.112

[Fig. 15] **Ernest Hébrard. Diocletian Palace in Split, 4th century AD. Reconstruction of original plan. 1912**

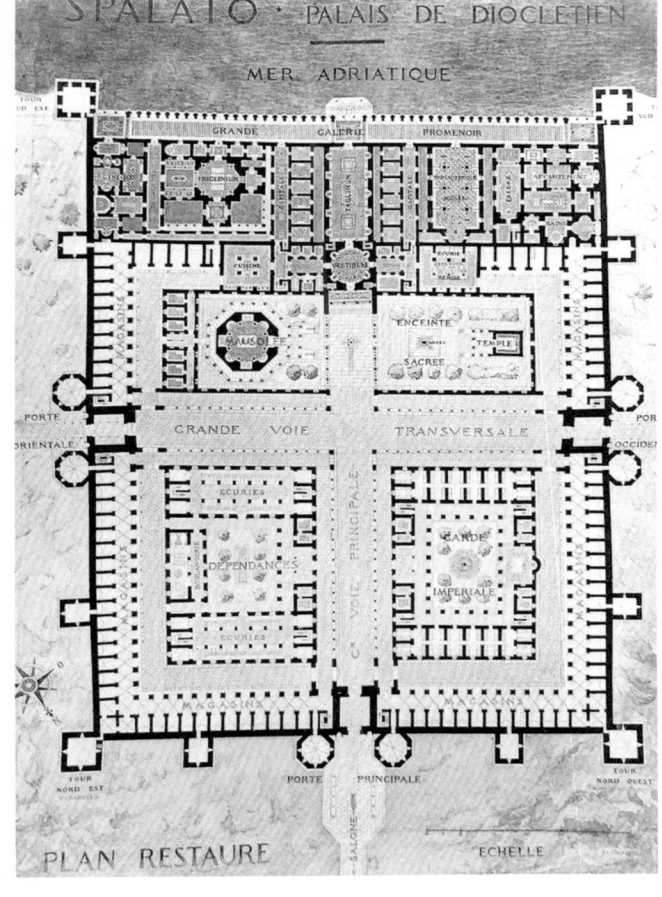

[Fig. 16] **Ernest Hébrard. Diocletian Palace in Split, Remains 1912. 1912**

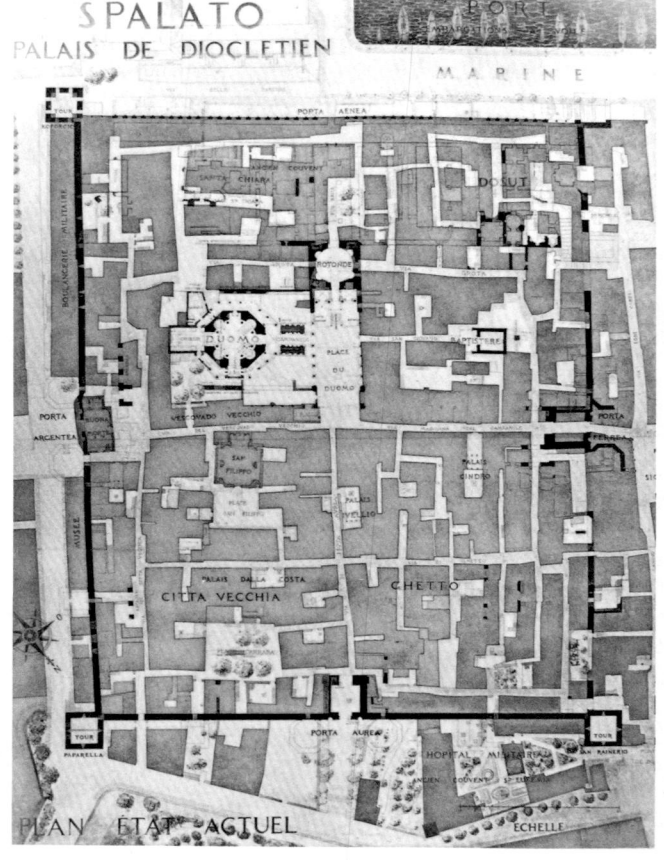

teriors become the city. Processes of topological deformations constructed over centuries from the scale of the public building into domestic interiors were codified by Aldo Rossi in his influential book *The Architecture of the City*, first published in 1966. Elaborating on examples of infrastructure converted into assemblages of history and architecture, Rossi coins the concept of 'urban artefacts' as primary elements whose existence guides the morphological and cultural evolution of the city.[28] In the case of the Diocletian Palace (originally a 4th-century Roman fortress), today it forms the city centre of the old town of Split, in a long-term, evolutionary displacement from palace to city, from public interior to urban fabric. Before the 20th century, these displacements could be grasped considering architectural tectonics as medium themselves. Architecture, to put it simply, *always had the form of architecture.*

---

28   Rossi, 1982, p.20-27

3

THINKING IN
THE EXPANDED MEDIA

'For, within the situation of postmodernism, practice is not defined in relation to a given medium—sculpture—but rather in relation to the logical operations on a set of cultural terms, for which any medium—photography, books, lines on walls, mirrors, or sculpture itself—might be used.'[29]

Rosalind Krauss

---

29 Krauss, 1979, p.42

In the late 1970s, art critic Rosalind Krauss explored in her seminal article, 'Sculpture in the Expanded Field,' the epistemology of sculpture at a time when its very existence seemed to assemble, for the first time in history, a large number of disparate mediums and disciplines, redefining the boundaries of architecture and landscape.[30] After briefly describing the successive emancipation of sculpture from the podium, its progressive sitelessness, ubiquity, and the diversity of practices of artists such as Mary Miss or Robert Smithson, Krauss rapidly enters into a discourse of affirmation by absences, her interest shifting to the terms *not-landscape* and *not-architecture*. For Krauss, at that time, landscape and architecture were sources of disciplinary stability.

Not-landscape, not-architecture > sculpture

The article was written before the fields of architecture and landscape had undergone the epistemic transformation of recent decades, themselves becoming as elastic as sculpture itself. Without entering the complexities of the scheme that defines the boundaries between the three

---

30 The impact of such redefinition was explored in 2014 in a series of round-table discussions involving intellectuals and critics in the three disciplines, such as Stan Allen, George Baker, Yves-Alain Bois, Benjamin Buchloh, Beatriz Colomina, Anthony Vidler, and Mary Miss, among others. See: Papapetros and Rose, 2014.
31 Krauss, *op.cit.*, p.42
32 Colomina, *op. cit.*, p.14

disciplines (the third step of its iteration being arguably the most discussed diagram in the history of art theory), what the article describes is an expanded field that Krauss characterises as belonging to the postmodern ethos.

It is interesting to note that Krauss uses the word medium in the singular and plural—never media—throughout her essay and that she critically associates this with a radical difference from the modern period, which she identifies as 'the modernist demand for the purity and separateness of the various mediums.'[31] Her position contrasts with that of Colomina, who in *Privacy and Publicity* literally argues 'that modern architecture only becomes modern with its engagement with the media.'[32] This contrast becomes more relevant if one considers that Colomina writes within the architectural field, a discipline whose very idea has been for centuries embedded into its physical existence, which she contests. Meanwhile, Krauss writes within the arts field during the very process of its disentanglement from the idea of medium.

As a leading intellectual figure, Krauss witnessed—and constructed—the transition in the 1980s from art as a medium-specific domain to the post-medium era, where the relationship between the technical (or material) support of art genres and the cultural conventions within which they operate started to be explored in manifold directions, a shift she associated with postmodernism. Whether our inhabitation of contempo-

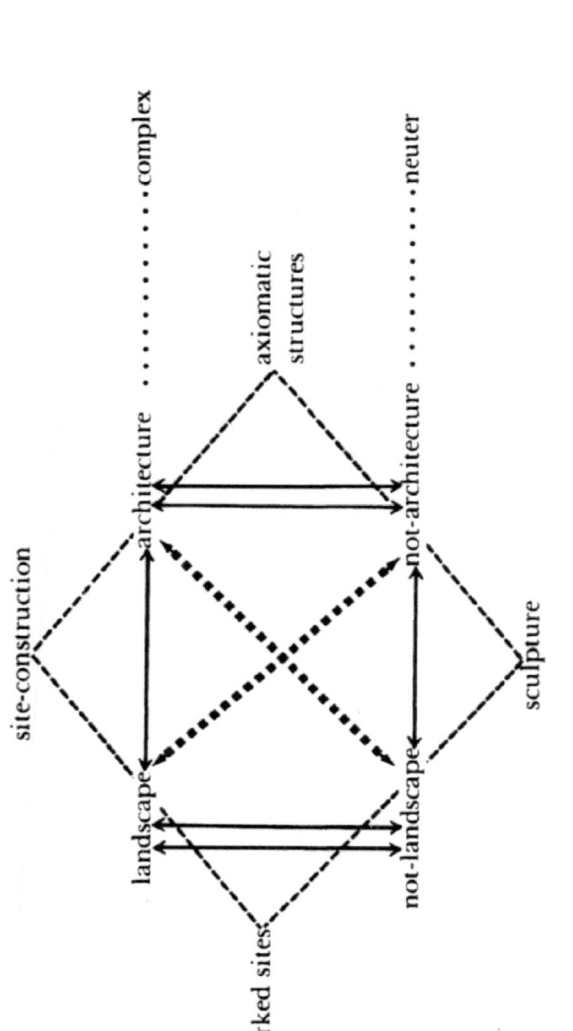

raneity is postmodern, or whether it belongs to a late state of modernity—'liquid' according to Zygmunt Bauman and other philosophers—is a debate in itself.[33] What is clear is that the transversal use of different mediums and media previously explained in Picasso and Le Corbusier show expanded fields of operation and practice in art and architecture that extend through the 20th century into contemporaneity.

The tension arising from the repetitive use of the terms 'medium/s' by Krauss and 'media' by Colomina is the very tension of the episteme of contemporary architecture. Even though representation in its most varied textual and graphic forms has never been neutral, the multiplicity of formats and media incorporated in the architectural medium in recent decades represents one of the most radical epistemological transformations the discipline of space design has ever seen. It has fundamentally created a new way of relational thinking, where spaces are hubs articulating larger physical and virtual domains. What we witness is an expansion of the mechanisms triggered in the beginning of the last century with the progressive addition of new systems of representation that endlessly pollute each other in infinite combinations. This is radically important to understanding the condition of contemporary interiors.

33 Bauman, *op. cit.*

In the eyes of the bed-holder
New York City, effect of Airbnb host and apartment characteristics on rental price, %

Negative effect ← | → Positive effect

Host characteristics
- Smile intensity*
- Attractiveness†
- Superhost
- Male*
- Age*
- Asian*
- Trustworthiness†
- Black*

No statistically significant effect (Superhost, Male, Age, Asian)

Apartment characteristics
- Median local rent
- Bedrooms
- Review score
- Number of reviews

*Assessed by algorithm
†Assessed by Mechanical Turk recruits

Source: "The effects of facial attractiveness and trustworthiness in online peer-to-peer markets" by Bastian Jaeger et al., *Journal of Economic Psychology*, 2019

It is a new scenario where the discussion about tectonics, material finishes, conditioning, energy consumption, furniture design, colour codes, and aesthetics go hand in hand with information, slogans, and dystopias such as:

- 'Airbnb users pay more to stay with an attractive host.'[34]
- '98% of the people depicted in the IKEA catalogue are young. 92% of them are blond.'[35]

Where the first sentence comes from a 2019 news item in *The Economist*, the second is from a 2011 project by architect Andrés Jaque, *IKEA Disobedients*. What this represents is a radical shift in the way societies are being constructed, where human beings become actors who cannot disengage their inhabitation from their performance in space. In the case of IKEA, the research carried out by Jaque refers to fabricated forms of domesticity where fiction is presented as reality. Its catalogue is not a transparent, neutral representation of how to use furniture, but rather an edulcorated construction of society through interiors. As the author claims, 'IKEA delivers societies,' to subsequently add, 'Not all of us are healthy. Not all of us are young. Not all of us are into having children.'[36] As for

34 'Airbnb users pay more to stay with attractive hosts,' *The Economist*, December 30, 2019
35 *IKEA Disobedients* (Madrid 2011; MoMA New York 2012), Andrés Jaque / Office for Political Innovation, https://vimeo.com/67141899
36 *Ibid.*

[Fig. 18] 'Airbnb users pay more to stay with attractive hosts,' *The Economist*, December 30, 2019

Thinking in the Expanded Media

Airbnb, not only must spaces be functional, clean, and likeable, so too must their users. This implies that peer-to-peer marketplaces are spatialised as beauty contests unfolding through interiors. In the survey, conducted in New York City, aspects such as age or gender prove not to be statistically significant, whereas black race or 'smile intensity' have, respectively, a negative and positive effect on rental price as a form of digital discrimination.

It is interesting to note that both quotes are dystopian, yet one comes from reality, the other from fiction. This is creating a world of exponential flatness where the images shared and circulated through millions of screens are assembled in a perpetual lack of context, depth, and specificity. The institutionalisation of social media in recent years has exacerbated this flatness. In the book *Instagram and Contemporary Image*, published in 2017, Lev Manovich analyses 16 million Instagram photographs shared in seventeen global cities between 2012 and 2016. After claiming that Instagram is a medium of its own, the author categorises three types of photographs shared by users: *casual, professional, and designed*. Whereas the lines between professional and designed types are sometimes blurry, as both appertain to 'competitive photography'—competing for likes, shares, and impact—the first type belongs to ordinary users, constructed in an infinite bottom-up process.[37]

37 Manovich, 2015-2017

[Fig. 19] IKEA Catalogue, 2011

Thinking in the Expanded Media

city	Body and people	food and drinks	clothing and accessories	nature	architecture	furniture
Tokyo	19.0	49.6	12.7	18.0	15.5	28.9
São Paulo	25.8	11.9	21.8	16.5	12.9	14.8
Moscow	22.0	8.4	15.2	25.0	21.1	19.5
Berlin	15.3	12.4	9.9	28.4	39.7	24.2
Bangkok	18	17.7	40.3	12.2	10.8	12.6

It would be expected that in casual photographs asymmetries arise among different geographies, cultures, and identities, yet in macro figures these asymmetries are percentage- not topic-based. As explained in the chapter, 'The Subjects of Casual Photos,' categories such as 'body and people', 'food and drinks', 'clothing and accessories', 'nature', 'architecture', and 'furniture' repeat across different locations and temporalities. Whereas Tokyo takes up 49.6% of the 'food and drinks' category, in Berlin the largest percentage goes to 'architecture'.[38] And yet the same categories remain: visually speaking, space is being consumed as food. What this announces is a world with a simultaneous eagerness to explore local specificities and a recurrent inability to grasp them. It is very telling that this condition belongs to what experts call the 'home mode', a term coined by Richard Chalfen in 1987 to refer to a way of communication by which users typically share content—photographs, video footage—of traditional subjects such as birthdays or holidays and 'know the people in the images'.[39]

The Covid crisis has forcefully put into circulation the largest quantity of domestic interiors ever seen. As opposed to theatre sets, cinema decors, or YouTube domestic-like scenes, these are interiors that were never envisioned as fictions. Through their

[Fig. 20] Lev Manovich and Miriam Redi. Computational analysis of subjects of 20,000 Instagram photos shared in Bangkok, Berlin, Moscow, São Paulo, and Tokyo from December 5 to 11, 2013

38   Ibid, p.64-67
39   Ibid, p.30-40

Thinking in the Expanded Media

instant reshaping as remote offices, ubiquitous gyms, assembled party rooms, or ready-made restaurants, they propose *a city of interiors,* an endless accumulation of rooms that are connected in the way they are successively performed, switched on and switched off. This is an understanding of the urban condition where the dominance of the plan through navigation tools, the objectualisation of buildings from bird's-eye views or the exteriority of façades are no longer sufficient to visualise what we understand by 'city'.

At the start of this essay, Magritte's quote refers to the capacity of painting to articulate the relationship between objects and words, things and thinking, through representation. We inhabit a pictorial moment, understanding the pictorial as not medium-specific, in the way the surface of representation, with its endless capacity to assemble fiction and reality, is fundamentally reshaping the episteme of space design. Architecture has a long tradition of obliterating human presence in its representation. People are not normally represented in plans or sections, and their recurrent role in models is to give scale. Examples of this absence in architectural photography are countless. History books rarely refer to human behavior, not to mention emotions, when describing interior spaces. But in media that are not specifically architectural, from cinema to commercial magazines, painting to literature, human beings are in most cases right at the centre of the image, the narrative, or the frame. Objects and spaces surround them, they do not displace them. *Thinking in the Expanded Media*, in this sense, means a capacity to develop a holistic understanding of interiors in all its mediated versions.

This is not a teleology of media as an end in itself, nor a substitution of space's physicality with the non-physical, but rather a new logic of articulation; an expanded playground where disciplinary challenges are addressed. This means understanding that contemporary interiors simultaneously belong to different places and temporalities, whether physical or virtual, close or distant. And envisioning a new reality that bypasses traditional distinctions such as public/private, past/present, tangible/mediated, or autonomous/iterated, legitimising the agency of space beyond physicality and reasserting the role of interior architecture in the construction of contemporaneity.

Manifesto of Interiors should not be seen as a closed statement but rather as an open hypothesis from which to move forward. The examples discussed are operative platforms for developing new glossaries that will be circulated as samples, fragments, and tools for the discipline of interiors. Since the end of the 19th century and remarkably into the 21st century, we have seen a hyperbolic acceleration in the amount and diversity of media, with the economic and societal implications this has had in terms of externalisation of privacy and mediatisation of all aspects of life, which have significantly disrupted the domain of interiors as episteme and practice. What we are witnessing today is not just an array of space types, it is an endless hybridisation of typologies through various media. There is a continuous increase in the number of design practices dealing with the production of space, and the absence of clear boundaries between them turns interior architecture into a relational and multidimensional practice by definition. The future is interiors.

Manifesto of Interiors

Brejzek, Thea, and Wallen, Lawrence, *The Model as Performance: Staging Space in Theatre and Architecture* (London: Bloomsbury Publishing, 2018)

David Hockney: Secret Knowledge, directed by Randall Wright (BBC Production, 2001)

Evans, Robin, *The Projective Cast: Architecture and Its Three Geometries* (Cambridge: The MIT Press, 1995)

Foucault, Michel, *This is not a Pipe* [1973] (Los Angeles: University of California Press, 1983)

Gitelman, Lisa, *Always Already New: Media, History and the Data of Culture* (Cambridge: The MIT Press, 2006)

Hockney, David, *Secret Knowledge: Rediscovering the Lost Techniques of the Old Masters* [2001] (London: Thames & Hudson, 2006)

McLuhan, Marshall, *Understanding Media: The Extensions of Man* (New York: McGraw-Hill, 1964)

Laboratories of Modernity

Bauman, Zygmunt, *Liquid Modernity* (Cambridge: Polity Press, 2000)

Colomina, Beatriz, *Privacy and Publicity: Modern Architecture as Mass Media* (Cambridge: The MIT Press, 1994)

Contreras, Javier F., *The Miralles Projection: Thinking and Representation in the Architecture of Enric Miralles* (New York: Applied Research + Design Publishing, 2020)

Evans, Robin, 'The Developed Surface' in *Translations from Drawing to Building* (London: Architectural Association Publications, 1997), p.195-232

Franklin, Adrian. *The tourist syndrome: An interview with Zygmunt Bauman. Tourist studies* vol. 3.2 (2003), p.205-217

Guillerme, Jacques, and Vérin, Hélène, 'The Archaeology of Section' in *Perspecta* Vol.25 (1989), p.226-257

Harris, John, *Moving Rooms: The Trade in Architectural Salvages* (New Haven: Yale University Press, 2007)

Johnson, Philip C., *Mies van der Rohe* (New York: The Museum of Modern Art, 1947)

Koolhaas, Rem, 'Transformations' in *A+U OMA Special Issue*, May 2000, p.106-115

Miralles, Enric, and Prats, Eva, 'How to Lay Out a

Croissant. Horizontal Equilibrium' in *El Croquis*, n°. 49/50 (Summer 1991), p.240-241

Moon, Iris, 'Hide-and-seek' in *Drawing Matter*, November 2019, [https://www.drawingmatter.org/sets/drawing-week/hide-and-seek/]

Richards, Jonathan, *Facadism* (London and New York: Routledge, 1994)

Rojo, Luis, 'La realidad en fragmentos [conflictos y palimpsestos]' in *Le Corbusier y el surrealismo: Paris 1920-1930* (Buenos Aires: Diseño, 2015), p.278-370

Rossi, Aldo, *The Architecture of the City* [1966] (Cambridge: The MIT Press, 2002)

Sánchez García, José María, *El caso Bath* (PhD dissertation, ETSAM, 2016), http://oa.upm.es/43854/1/JOSE_MARIA_SANCHEZ_GARCIA_1.pdf

Sparke, Penny, *The Modern Interior* (London: Reaktion Books, 2008)

Thinking in the Expanded Media

'Airbnb users pay more to stay with attractive hosts' in *The Economist*, December 30, 2019, https://www.economist.com/graphic-detail/2019/12/30/airbnb-users-pay-more-to-stay-with-attractive-hosts

IKEA Disobedients (Madrid 2011; MoMA New York 2012), Andrés Jaque / Office for Political Innovation, https://vimeo.com/67141899

Krauss, Rosalind, 'Sculpture in the Expanded Field' in *October*, Vol.8. (Spring 1979), p.30-44

Manovich, Lev, *Instagram and Contemporary Image* (self-pub., 2015-2017) [http://manovich.net/index.php/projects/instagram-and-contemporary-image]

Papapetros, Spyros, and Rose, Julian, (eds.), *Retracing the Expanded Field: Encounters between Art and Architecture* (Cambridge: The MIT Press, 2014)

HEAD – Publishing, 2021

Texts published under free license CC BY–SA

Title: *Manifesto of Interiors: Thinking in the Expanded Media*

Author: Javier Fernández Contreras

Manifestes collection edited by Julie Enckell Julliard and Anthony Masure

Editorial coordinator: Sylvain Menétrey

Proofreading: Stephanie O'Dea

Manifestes collection designed by Dimitri Broquard

Fonts: ABC Whyte (Dinamo, 2019), Lyon Text (Commercial Type, 2009)

Printed by Artgraphic Cavin SA

ISBN: 978-2-940510-45-0

Legal deposit: March 2021

[Fig. 1]: The Metropolitan Museum of Art, Open Access. Accession Number: 41.100.126-(2.19)

[Fig. 2]: Photo: Lawrence Wallen, 2015

[Fig. 3]: M Leuven, www.artinflanders.be, photo Hugo Maertens

[Fig. 4]: Attributed to Bramante, from 'The Archaeology of Section' by Jacques Guillerme, Hélène Vérin, and Stephen Sartarelli, in Perspecta, Vol. 25 (1989), p. 226-257, reprinted courtesy of The MIT Press on behalf of Perspecta

[Fig. 5]: Courtesy of Drawing Matter

[Fig. 6]: © Succession Picasso / 2020, ProLitteris, Zurich pour les œuvres de PICASSO PABLO

[Fig. 7]: © Succession Picasso / 2020, ProLitteris, Zurich pour les œuvres de PICASSO PABLO

[Fig. 8]: *The Seven Year Itch*, Fair Use

[Fig. 9]: Interfoto / Alamy Stock Photo, Image ID: BR62MH

[Fig. 10]: Collection Kröller-Müller Museum, Otterlo, The Netherlands

[Fig. 11]: Mies van der Rohe Archive, gift of the architect. Catalogue number MMA1811. New York, Museum of Modern Art (MoMA). © 2020. Digital image Mies van der Rohe/Gift of the Arch./MoMA/Scala

[Fig. 12]: Fundació Enric Miralles, Barcelona

[Fig. 13]: Image courtesy OMA

[Fig. 14]: Image courtesy OMA

[Fig. 15]: Public Domain

[Fig. 16]: Public Domain

[Fig. 17]: Krauss, Rosalind E., *The Originality of the Avant-Garde and Other Modernist Myths*, figure, p.283, © 1985 Massachusetts Institute of Technology, by permission of The MIT Press

[Fig. 18]: © The Economist Group Limited, London (Dec 30, 2019)

[Fig. 19]: Inter IKEA Systems BV

[Fig. 20]: Lev Manovich. Creative Commons

Image credits

Javier Fernández Contreras (Dipl. ETSAM 2006, PhD 2013) is an architect, critic and the dean of the Department of Interior Architecture at HEAD – Genève. His work explores the relationship between architecture, representation and media, with a specific focus on the role of interiors in the construction of contemporaneity. He is the author of the books *Fragmentos de Planta y Espacio* (Ediciones Asimétricas, 2018) and *The Miralles Projection* (Applied Research and Design, 2020). His critical essays have been published in different specialised books and journals, including *Massilia Annuaire des Études Corbuséennes, Marie-José Van Hee Architecten, Perspectives in Metropolitan Research, 306090, Drawing Matter, RA Revista de Arquitectura.*